HERO of the High Seas

JOHN PAUL JONES
AND THE AMERICAN REVOLUTION

by Michael L. Cooper

NATIONAL GEOGRAPHIC

WASHINGTON, D.C.

To my brother, Ron Cooper

Published by the National Geographic Society.

Book design by David M. Seager
Carl Mehler, *Director of Maps* Matt Chwastyk, *Map Research and Production*
The body and display text of the book is set in Incognito.

Printed in the United States

Acknowledgments

Special thanks to James Cheevers at the U.S. Naval Academy Museum and Archives for his help with the photographs and illustrations. And thanks once again to Sharon Shelton, a longtime English and writing teacher (she's also my aunt) at Whitley County (KY) High School for her valuable comments on the manuscript as well as her expert proofreading and copyediting skills. And thanks to Mike Duniven for his encouragement and helpful comments on the manuscript.

For information about special discounts for bulk purchases,
please contact National GeographicBooks Special Sales: ngspecales@ngs.org

Library of Congress Cataloging-in-Publication Data
Cooper, Michael L., 1950-
Hero of the high seas : John Paul Jones and the American Revolution / by Michael L. Cooper.   p. cm.
Includes bibliographical references and index.
Trade ISBN 10: 0-7922-5547-X Library ISBN 10: 0-7922-5548-8
Trade ISBN 13: 978-0-7922-5547-5 Library ISBN 13: 978-0-7922-5548-2
1. Jones, John Paul, 1747-1792--Juvenile literature. 2. Admirals--United States--Biography--Juvenile literature. 3. United States. Navy--Biography--Juvenile literature. 4. United States--History--Revolution, 1775-1783--Naval operations--Juvenile literature.
I. Title.   E207.J7C58 2006   973.3'5092--dc22

2005036256

Contents

Foreword 6

Introduction 9

◦ *Foreword* ◦

HERMAN MELVILLE, an American author, described John Paul Jones as "intrepid, unprincipled, reckless, predatory, with boundless ambition, civilized in external but a savage at heart," and any discriminating historian would have to agree. Jones is properly credited as the man whose maritime exploits helped win the Revolutionary War, but his fiery personality is often overlooked.

Hero of the High Seas illustrates Jones as brave, dutiful, and glorious, but also as exceedingly daring and ambitious to a fault. While some of Jones's traits do not fit our romantic ideals of a hero,

I challenge you to show me someone flawless who has made a significant contribution to history. It is not perfection that characterizes greatness. It is, rather, the ability to achieve great things in spite of our weaknesses.

Jones became an American icon by virtue of a uniquely American pursuit: self-invention. He came from class-bound Britain, where he could hope to be little more than the son of a gardener. It was in America that he determined exactly who he wanted to be. This nation gave his ambition opportunity, and he used that opportunity to gain fame and stature. The gardener's son became a celebrated war hero.

Those who serve in the Navy are diligently taught the history of the complex man called John Paul Jones, with all his virtues, faults, and foibles. I regret, for most young students, his legacy is often reduced to just a few dry sentences in a textbook. However, those who read Michael Cooper's rich biography will discover the exciting true story of the man who pioneered the proud tradition of the American Navy.

John McCain

United States Senator, U.S. Navy 1954–1981

You have heard o' Paul Jones,
Have you not, Have you not?
And you've heard of Paul Jones,
Have you not?

HIS SCOTS BALLAD FROM TWO HUNDRED years ago is about a famous sea captain we know as John Paul Jones. He is the Revolutionary War naval hero who supposedly yelled, "I have not yet begun to fight!" at a British Navy captain who asked Jones if he was surrendering during a battle between the American ship *Bonhomme Richard* and the British ship *Serapis.*

I say "supposedly" because historians don't believe he said those exact words. The phrase has survived through the

The famous and bloody sea battle between Serapis *and* Bonhomme Richard

° 9 °

years because it appeared in the first biography of the captain, John Henry Sherburne's *Life and Character of the Chevalier John Paul Jones* (New York: Wilder & Campbell, 1825).

But, I hasten to add, although Jones might not have said those words, they do reflect his spirit. He was an aggressive, determined man. Jones won his battle that day against a larger, better-armed ship. The four-hour fight between the *Bonhomme Richard* and the *Serapis* was the biggest naval battle of the American Revolution. The victory made Captain Jones famous in the United States and in Europe.

John Paul Jones openly sought fame. "My desire for fame is infinite," he once wrote. With no television, movies, or recording industry, the methods of gaining fame were limited in that era. Jones chose an age-old path–military service.

By using his naval skills during the American Revolution, the Scots immigrant intended to prove himself a man of courage, integrity, and honor. With fame honorably gained, Jones hoped to find a home among America's most respected men. This is the story of how John Paul Jones became an American hero.

An engraving of John Paul Jones based on a portrait by the famous Revolutionary-era painter Charles Wilson Peale

CHAPTER ONE

The Greatest Misfortune

THE MAN KNOWN AS JOHN PAUL JONES was actually named John Paul. But the sea captain changed his name after a tragic fight on a Caribbean island caused him to flee to America just as the War for Independence was starting.

In January 1773, John Paul was captain of the *Betsy* when it sailed from Plymouth, England, carrying a cargo of wine, butter, and oats. The merchant ship was bound for the British colony of Tobago, a Caribbean island near South America. The captain had spent half of his 26 years at sea and crossed the

This drawing from an old map depicts a Caribbean port.

Atlantic Ocean many times. But this trip was more troublesome than any other.

The *Betsy* "proved so very leakey," Paul wrote in his log, "that it was with the greatest difficulty that we could keep her free with both pumps." All sailing ships leaked, but this leak nearly sank the boat. The day after leaving England, the captain sought safe harbor in Cork, Ireland. Carpenters inspected the vessel and found 30 broken futtocks. These curved timbers are like a ship's ribs. The repairs required six months.

That summer, with a new cargo, the *Betsy* resumed its voyage and ten weeks later sailed into the harbor at Scarborough, Tobago's main town. A few hundred British people lived on the island, overseeing sugar plantations worked by thousands of African slaves.

Soon after the *Betsy* dropped anchor, the fight occurred that Paul called "the greatest misfortune of my life." Several crewmen wanted to visit family and friends onshore, so they asked for their salary. But Captain Paul said no. He wanted to keep all of his cash to buy local molasses, a black syrup made from sugar cane. He planned to sell the molasses in the British colony of Virginia and

then purchase tobacco and other products to sell
in England. Then, at the end of the voyage, he
would pay the crew. Cursing and complaining, the
sailors accepted the decision, but still wanted to
go ashore. Paul again said no.

It is not clear why he refused to let the sailors
go ashore. Perhaps Paul felt that he needed to be
tough with his crew. He was a young captain and
sailors could be hard to supervise. But Paul's
tough behavior backfired. The men became even
angrier. Paul described the incident three years
later in a letter to Benjamin Franklin. He called
one of the angry crewmen the "Ringleader." The
Ringleader was a "prodigious brute of thrice my
strength," Paul explained in his letter, who shouted
"the grossest abuse that vulgarism could dictate."
The captain, a thin man barely five-and-a-half feet
tall, was no match for this sailor. He retreated to
his cabin and grabbed his sword.

When the captain emerged from his cabin
with his sword drawn, the Ringleader became more
enraged. He attacked Paul with a short club called a
bludgeon. As the sailor was about to crush his skull
with the bludgeon, the captain thrust his sword
deep into the man's stomach. The Ringleader's

William H. Myers, a sailor in the early 19th century, sketched this scene of a flogging aboard his ship, the USS Cyane.

anger turned to shock as he screamed, clutched
his bloody wound, and collapsed on the deck.
He died within minutes.

Captain Paul went ashore to report the death.
This kind of case would normally go to Admiralty
Court. But that court was not in session, so Paul
expected to face a jury in civil court. His business
partner and the *Betsy's* co-owner, Archibald
Stuart, lived on Tobago. Stuart warned Paul that
he might not get a fair trial because the dead
man's relatives and friends would be on the jury.
This predicament probably reminded Paul of the
time four years earlier when he had been arrested
for murder.

That incident had begun during a voyage to the
Caribbean when he flogged his lazy and insolent
ship's carpenter, Mungo Maxwell. Flogging in
those days was common punishment for offenses
both minor and major. The offender would be
stripped to the waist and tied to the ship's rigging.
Then, the captain or one of his officers would
whip the man. They often used a cat-o'-nine-tails,
a whip made of nine tightly wound and knotted
lengths of either cord or leather. A dozen lashes
was the typical punishment for minor offenses.

The cat-o'-nine-tails, according to one account, left a man's back looking like "roasted meat burnt nearly black before a scorching fire."

A few weeks after the beating, Maxwell died of malaria. This disease, which is spread by mosquitoes, plagued sailors in the tropics. But Maxwell's father blamed Paul for his son's death and a sheriff arrested the captain when he returned to his homeport of Whitehaven, England. Several months later, after witnesses stated that the flogging had not killed Maxwell, the court had dropped the murder charge.

Perhaps that incident taught Paul how hard it could be to defend oneself against such a serious charge. It would be especially difficult on a remote island before a jury of the dead man's friends and relatives. No one knows exactly why Captain Paul decided to flee Tobago. But he entrusted the *Betsy* and its cargo to Stuart and boarded a ship bound for Virginia under the new name of John Jones.

A cat-o'-nine-tails, a whip used to discipline sailors in the 18th and early 19th centuries

Eve of Revolution

JOHN JONES ARRIVED IN THE COLONIES of British North America at a bad time. After years of accumulating grievances, the colonists were on the brink of rebellion against Great Britain. But Jones was too absorbed in his own affairs to immediately notice the militant mood.

The sea captain traveled to Virginia to visit his older and only brother, William Paul. William had left their home in southwest Scotland as a teenager, some 20 years earlier. He emigrated to Fredericksburg, Virginia, a prosperous village on the

Paul Revere created this engraving of Boston Harbor in 1744.

south shore of the Rappahannock River. It was the county seat and a busy river port for exporting tobacco, Virginia's main crop in the colonial era. Many of the town's merchants were Scotsmen. William was a well-to-do tailor.

John had first visited his brother in the summer of 1764, on his maiden voyage as a sailor's apprentice, or ship's boy. "America was my favorite country from the age of 13, when I first saw it," he noted years later in a letter. He especially liked Virginia, which was the oldest, richest, and biggest of the 13 colonies. Some 500,000 people, one-fifth of British America's entire population, lived in Virginia. The colony seemed to offer the young man more opportunities than he had back home in Scotland.

The Paul brothers and their three sisters grew up in a two-room cottage on an estate called Arbigland, near the town of Kirkcudbright, in southwest Scotland. Their father and mother worked on the estate as gardener and housekeeper. John grew up determined to become a wealthy and respected man. After attending the local Presbyterian parish school for several years, with his father's help, John went to work on a ship

owned by a merchant in Whitehaven, a busy
English port on the Irish Sea about 20 miles
(32 km) south of Kirkcudbright.

    The teenager sailed from the British Isles to
Africa, to the Caribbean islands, and to North
America. He learned about rigging, winds, ocean
currents, navigation, and the many other skills
needed to sail a vessel. John quickly worked his
way up to second mate and then to first mate.
By age 24, he was captain of his own ship. It was
unusual for a man so young to become a ship's
captain. Many merchant ship captains became
wealthy carrying goods between the British Isles
and the British colonies. John appeared to be on

The house where John Paul Jones was born in southern Scotland is now a museum dedicated to his life.

William Paul lived in Fredericksburg, Virginia.

his way to becoming a prosperous man, until he killed the sailor in Tobago.

Although the captain abandoned his ship and his family's name, he did not abandon his dreams. In Virginia, John Jones saw that prominent men like George Washington, Thomas Jefferson, and Patrick Henry lived in elegant houses on large farms called *plantations.* Jones decided he wanted to buy a Virginia plantation and live a life, he wrote in one letter, of "calm contemplation and poetic ease." A plantation in Virginia also would provide status and influence. He seemed

unbothered by the fact that slavery made plantation life possible. About half of Virginia's population was enslaved.

Jones arrived in Fredericksburg in December
1774 and found his brother gravely ill. The histor-
ical record does not name William's illness, but it
was obviously quite serious because the 37-year-
old man died by year's end. If Jones expected an
inheritance, he was disappointed. William and his
wife had separated. The separation complicated
William's estate, which was not settled until years
later. With little money to live on, the sea captain
needed a job.

Jones spent the first half of 1775 meeting
men who could help him. Seeking out people who
worked in the same or similar occupations was a
good way to find a job. He visited Edenton, a port
town on Albemarle Sound in eastern North
Carolina, to meet a fellow Scotsman, Robert Smith.
He was a partner in the shipping firm of Hewes &
Smith. But Mr. Smith had nothing to offer his
countryman. Transatlantic trade with Great Britain
had stopped. Merchant ships sat idle in the ports
because of a trade boycott by the colonies.

The boycott had begun in the fall of the previous

year. It was proposed by the 56 colonial representatives meeting in Philadelphia, Pennsylvania, for the First Continental Congress. They had gathered there to decide how to respond to the British decision to close Boston's port and suspend local government. Government ministers in London, Great Britain's capital, were punishing the Massachusetts colony because a group of Boston men, protesting a hated tea tax, had boarded three merchant ships on the night of December 16, 1773, and dumped a valuable cargo of tea into the harbor. This episode became known as the Boston Tea Party. The Continental Congress, after several weeks of discussion, voted to stop buying all British goods. It was a rare example of cooperation among the quarrelsome, independent-minded colonies, which often thought of themselves as individual states, or countries.

The feud at first did not concern Jones. After all, conflict was not unusual in Great Britain. The people of Scotland, a formerly independent kingdom that was part of Great Britain, had rebelled several times. Two years before Jones's birth, an army of Scots had fought its way to the outskirts of London before being brutally crushed.

The rebellion is remembered in Scotland's history as "the Rising of 1745."

When Jones returned to Virginia from North Carolina, he expanded his social network. He joined the Fredericksburg Lodge of the Ancient Society of Free and Accepted Masons, a fraternal order of white, Protestant men. The monthly concerts and balls at the local lodge gave the captain opportunities to meet prominent people. Jones soon became friends with Dr. John K. Read, a nephew of Benjamin Franklin's wife. Like Jones, Read was a Scotsman in his mid-20s. He lived at the Grove, a plantation between Fredericksburg and Richmond, Virginia.

Jones frequently visited the Grove. On one visit the doctor introduced the sea captain to Martha Washington's cousin, Dorothea Dandridge. She lived on her family's plantation in nearby Goochland County.

It's doubtful that Dorothea's parents were pleased by Jones's interest in their 19-year-old daughter. America was less class-conscious than Europe, but class still mattered. Few Virginia planters would welcome the unemployed son of a Scottish gardener into their family. Dorothea's parents probably preferred another suitor, Patrick Henry. Virginians knew this lawyer and politician as a dramatic and forceful voice against Britain. He was long remembered for a single sentence from a passionate speech in March 1775, "Give me liberty or give me death." Henry, a widower and father of six children, eventually married Dorothea.

Jones never married, although by all accounts he was a "ladies' man," popular with women. The captain was a handsome man, slender with short auburn hair, hazel eyes, a sharp nose, thin lips, and a cleft chin. His only flaw, and it was really too minor to call a flaw, was a slightly misshapen earlobe.

The sea captain spent weeks at a time at the Grove. He and Read probably discussed the ideas that were popular among colonial leaders and inspired the rebellion against British rule. They would have talked about the dangers of absolute power, or tyranny, and of the need for safeguards against tyranny. And the pair probably talked about "natural aristocrats," self-made men who earned their reputations and wealth, rather than inheriting them like a British king or duke.

Meanwhile, farther north, the conflict with Great Britain grew deadlier. In April, a daylong battle in the Massachusetts villages of Lexington and Concord near Boston left nearly 300 British soldiers dead or wounded.

The growing violence led colonial delegates to convene in Philadelphia on May 10, 1775, for the Second Continental Congress. Some 30,000 people lived in British America's largest, wealthiest, and most beautiful city, which sprawled along the western shore of the wide Delaware River. Despite being 100 miles (160 km) from the ocean, it was America's busiest port. Some two miles (over 3 km) of wharf crowded with frigates, sloops, and brigs lined the river. Philadelphia had an elegance lacking in Boston, Richmond, and other colonial cities. Brick walks and gutters lined the streets near the wharf. At night, whale oil lamps lit the streets. The city's many grand buildings included Carpenter's Hall, Christ Church, and the Pennsylvania State House.

The Second Continental Congress convened in the State House, a two-story redbrick building with a large clock on the exterior of the west wall, a tall bell tower, and one-story wings on either end. The building, which still stands today, is now called Independence Hall.

On June 14, the delegates resolved to create the American Continental Army. The following day, they appointed George Washington, the former commander of Virginia's militia, to be commander in chief of the new army. The armed conflict quickly became worse. In Massachusetts, 2,000 British soldiers attacked 1,500 colonial militiamen on Breed's Hill and neighboring Bunker Hill. The British captured the two hills, but a thousand of them were wounded or killed in the fight that became known as the Battle of Bunker Hill.

General Washington set up headquarters in Cambridge, Massachusetts, across the Charles River from British-occupied Boston. One of his first official acts was to arm eight New England fishing schooners. The British depended on ships to deliver supplies to their soldiers in North America, and Washington wanted his schooners to attack those supply ships. Washington's little navy soon proved its value by capturing the *Nancy*, which was carrying 2,000 muskets, 100,000 flints, 20,000 rounds of shot, and 60,000 pounds of musket balls.

The Continental Army had few military supplies. Before the Battle of Bunker Hill, militiamen

George Washington, several years before the Revolution, in a painting by Charles Wilson Peale, who painted many of the Founding Fathers.

had melted down iron church bells to make musket balls. When those ran out, they loaded their muskets with nails and pieces of iron. Britain had limited manufacturing in the colonies so that the colonists would have to buy all of their manufactured goods from England. The shortage of munitions became worse after King George III, Great Britain's ruling monarch, in October 1774 banned export of guns and powder to the colonies.

In the summer of 1775, Jones decided to go to Philadelphia, the capital of the revolutionary government. Through his friends, the captain had learned that Congress planned to create a navy, and there would be a need for ships' captains. This was his chance not only to find a job, but more important, to serve his adopted country. Jones knew that a distinguished and honorable military career would give him more opportunities than money could ever buy. It would help him become one of America's natural aristocrats.

Jones also decided once again to change his name. He never explained the reason for changing his name a second time. But when the captain reached Pennsylvania, he called himself John Paul Jones.

As usual, Jones immediately sought out men who might help him. He met Joseph Hewes, one of North Carolina's congressmen and the other business partner in Hewes & Smith. Hewes served on the Continental Congress's Naval Committee. The committee was in charge of creating the Continental Navy by obtaining ships, buying supplies, and appointing officers.

John Adams, a congressional delegate from Massachusetts, that fall introduced the resolution to establish the new navy. Congress approved his resolution on October 30, 1775. This is the official birthday of the U.S. Navy. Congress then created the marine soldiers, or simply marines, on November 10. This is the official birthday of the U.S. Marine Corps. Like their counterparts in European navies, the marines would serve on ships to provide musketry support in naval battles and to conduct land raids. The marines also would be a unified and disciplined force to prevent mutinies, or rebellions, aboard ships. Mutinies were commonplace in those days.

Two weeks later, influential friends secured Jones a commission as a lieutenant. He and his fellow officers now faced the daunting task of building a navy. 🚢

CHAPTER THREE

Building America's First Navy

THE CONTINENTAL NAVY BEGAN WITH NO warships, no men, and no money. Great Britain's Royal Navy, on the other hand, had 270 warships. Nearly half of them carried 50 or more guns. It was the strongest navy in the world. The well-disciplined British "tars," or sailors, expressed their confidence in boastful songs such as, "Two skinny Frenchmen and one Portugee / One British sailor can beat all three."

The Naval Committee immediately ordered the construction of 13 medium-size sailing ships, or frigates. But it would take

A modern oil painting depicts the American raid in the Bahamas.

carpenters a year or more to build them.
Meanwhile, the committee purchased five
merchantmen to convert to warships and assigned
Lt. John Paul Jones to oversee the conversion of
one of them, the 100-foot-long (30 m) *Alfred*.
Jones promptly went to work training a crew,
buying supplies, and hiring carpenters to cut gun
ports in the ship's wooden sides for 20 nine-
pound guns and ten six-pounders.

Cast-iron cannons were classed by the weight
of the roundballs they fired. A 16-pound cannon,
for example, fired a 16-pound ball. The cannons
could also fire links of chain or handfuls of
small iron balls called, because of their size,
grapeshot. The chain links and
grapeshot spread like buckshot from a
shotgun blast to shred an enemy's sails
and sever sheets, the ropes used to furl
or unfurl the sails.

Lieutenant Jones bought claw-shaped pieces of
iron called *grappling hooks*. These were tied to
ropes and thrown across the railing of an enemy
ship so it could be pulled near enough for armed
men to jump aboard. For close combat, Jones
bought short-barreled guns called *blunderbusses*,

Jones's sextant is now at the U.S. Naval Academy. The sextant was an important instrument for navigation during the era of sailing ships.

as well as muskets, pistols, cutlasses, hatchets, and pikes, which were like spears.

That winter, while waiting for the frozen Delaware River to thaw, the lieutenant kept his crew of 220 men and boys busy "exercising the guns." The rat-a-tat-tat of a drum, a signal called "beat to quarters," would summon the sailors to their battle stations. Each cannon had a crew of nine or ten men. Ship's boys, known as "powder monkeys," stacked cartridges next to each cannon. The cartridges were flannel bags filled with gunpowder. The chief gunner checked to see that each cannon had plenty of balls and cartridges and began barking orders.

"Cast loose your guns!"

The men untied the ropes that secured the heavy guns sitting on wheels. They were tied in place when not in use because a loose cannon rolling around the deck could cause a lot of damage.

"Take out your tampions!"

The crews pulled the *tampions*, or plugs, from the cannon muzzles.

"Load with cartridge!"

The gunners pushed the bags of powder down the muzzles.

"Shot your guns!"

They slid cannonballs into the barrels.

"Run out your guns!"

The men pushed the cannons' muzzles through the gun ports.

"Prime!"

The gun crews slid long metal pins through holes in the butt of the cannon to pierce the cloth cartridge and inserted fuses.

"Point your guns! Elevate!"

Aiming a cannon was tricky because the ship was swaying back and forth on the water. The chief waited until the vessel rolled nearly level with the target before yelling, "Fire!" The gunner then lit the fuse, and in less than a second it burned down to the powder and exploded.

"Sponge your guns!" the chief yelled as acrid-smelling, gray-yellow smoke filled the air. From nearby tubs of water, the crew grabbed poles tipped with sponges and rammed them down the hot cannon muzzles to extinguish pieces of burning cartridge bags. This routine took four to five minutes, depending on the skill of the crew.

In the February 1776, the *Alfred* and four other converted merchantmen–*Columbus*, *Cabot*,

The Alfred at anchor in the harbor at Philadelphia

Andrew Doria, and *Providence*–set out on their
first mission. "Was it proof of madness," Jones
later reflected, "to have at so critical a period
launched out on the ocean with only two armed
merchant ships, two armed brigantines, and one
armed sloop, to make war against such a power
as Great Britain?"

Friends and family of the Naval
Committee had received the Navy's top jobs.
The committee appointed Esek Hopkins,
brother of committee chairman Stephen
Hopkins, to be commander of the Continental
Navy. Dudley Saltonstall, the brother-in-law of
committee member Silas Deane, became captain
of the *Alfred*.

Jones complained about this nepotism, but he
had depended on influential friends, too. Thanks
to Joseph Hewes, the committee had offered him
command of the sloop *Providence*. Surprisingly,
Jones turned it down, explaining that he had never
sailed a single-mast sloop and sloops were hard to
handle. This explanation seems out of character
since Jones seldom doubted his abilities.

With Jones second in command on the *Alfred*,
the fleet of five ships sailed to New Providence, a

*The Continental
Congress appointed
Esek Hopkins,
a former privateer, as
the first commander
in chief of the
Continental Navy.*

British town on an island in the Bahamas, about 150 miles (250 km) east of Florida's southern tip. There the Americans captured an unguarded cache of 88 cannons, 11,000 cannonballs, and 24 casks of gunpowder. Jones later boasted in a letter that he "developed the plan" for the raid. But Hopkins never mentioned Jones in his official report, so the boast seems to be a bit of self-promotion.

The fleet sailed from the Bahamas back up the Atlantic coast. Near New York they met the British warship *Glasgow*, commanded by Capt. Tryingham Howe. The Royal Navy was blocking American ports to keep the rebels from receiving supplies from abroad.

The American drummers played "beat to quarters," and the sailors prepared for their first battle. When the *Glasgow* and the *Cabot* were within a hundred feet (30 m) of each other, a British sailor demanded to know if the *Cabot* was friend or foe. An American replied by throwing a grenade onto the *Glasgow*'s deck. The British ship immediately fired a broadside at the *Cabot*. The simultaneous firing of all the cannons on one side of a ship is called a *broadside*. The cannonfire wounded Capt. John Hopkins and killed the captain's mate and several sailors.

The *Alfred*, with Lieutenant Jones in charge of the nine-pound cannons, exchanged broadsides with the *Glasgow* until the British blew away the *Alfred*'s wheel block, making steering impossible. The ship drifted away from the battle, while the carpenters worked to repair the damage.

Then, the *Andrew Doria* sailed around to the *Glasgow*'s port, or left side, while the *Columbus* swung around to the *Glasgow*'s starboard, or the right side. The ships fought for three "glasses," an hour and a half. Sailors measured time with sand-filled half-hourglasses.

Captain Howe, flanked by the two ships, feared the Americans would grapple and board his vessel. He decided to run for it. The *Glasgow*'s rigging hung limply from its masts and its sails fluttered like rags in the wind, but it managed to escape to nearby Newport, a Rhode Island town occupied by the British.

A month later, on May 10, 1776, Commodore Hopkins promoted Jones to captain of the *Providence*. The Naval Committee court-martialed Captain Saltonstall for stealing stores, or supplies. Jones thought the *Alfred*'s captain was "ill

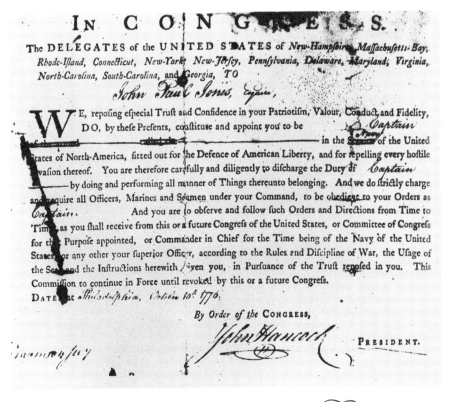

IN CONGRESS.

The DELEGATES of the UNITED STATES of *New-Hampshire, Massachusetts-Bay,*
Rhode-Island, Connecticut, New-York, New-Jersey, Pennsylvania, Delaware, Maryland, Virginia,
North-Carolina, South-Carolina, and *Georgia,* TO

John Paul Jones, Esquire,

WE, reposing especial Trust and Confidence in your Patriotism, Valour, Conduct, and Fidelity,
DO, by these Presents, constitute and appoint you to be *Captain*
——————————————————————————— in the *Navy* of the United
States of North-America, fitted out for the Defence of American Liberty, and for repelling every hostile
Invasion thereof. You are therefore carefully and diligently to discharge the Duty of *Captain*
——————— by doing and performing all manner of Things thereunto belonging. And we do strictly charge
and require all Officers, Marines and Seamen under your Command, to be obedient to your Orders as
Captain. And you are to observe and follow such Orders and Directions from Time to
Time as you shall receive from this or a future Congress of the United States, or Committee of Congress
for that Purpose appointed, or Commander in Chief for the Time being of the Navy of the United
States, or any other your superior Officer, according to the Rules and Discipline of War, the Usage of
the Sea and the Instructions herewith given you, in Pursuance of the Trust reposed in you. This
Commission to continue in Force until revoked by this or a future Congress.
DATED at *Philadelphia, October 10th 1776.*

By Order of the CONGRESS,

John Hancock PRESIDENT.

natured and narrow minded," and he gladly
accepted the promotion.

That summer the Continental Congress in
Philadelphia took decisive steps toward independence. "That these United Colonies are, and of
right ought to be, free and independent states,"
resolved Richard Henry Lee of Virginia, "absolved
from all allegiance to the British Crown...."

The order signed by
John Hancock, presi-
dent of the Continental
Congress, promoting
John Paul Jones to
captain

For two weeks Congress debated Lee's resolution. On July 1, John Adams of Massachusetts urged independence, Virginia delegate Thomas Jefferson wrote in his journal, "with power of thought and expression that moved us from our seats." The following morning, as a cloudburst filled Philadelphia's streets with rain, the delegates voted for independence.

The front page of the Pennsylvania *Evening Post* carried the full text of the Declaration of Independence on July 6, Jones's 29th birthday. By month's end, messengers on horseback had spread the news throughout the colonies. Not everyone wanted independence, however. Some 500,000 people, about one-fifth of the colonial population, were Tories, or British loyalists. Many left for British colonies in Canada. Others stayed, expecting Britain to easily crush the rebellion.

An official read the Declaration at noon on July 8 to an excited crowd in the State House yard. Six Philadelphians, specially chosen for the honor, removed the King's coat of arms from the State House and threw it onto a bonfire. A battery of cannons fired 13 blasts while five battalions of American troops paraded along the city's cobblestone streets. Church bells rang late into the night. People built bonfires on the street corners and lit candles in the windows of their homes. The city glowed with light and excitement.

While Philadelphia celebrated, hundreds of British ships appeared off the coast of New York. It looked as though "all London was afloat," remarked one awed colonist. The vessels carried 32,000 British and Hessian soldiers. The Hessians were German mercenaries. A mercenary is a soldier hired to fight in a foreign army. This was the largest army ever amassed by Britain at that time.

Having evacuated Boston five months earlier, the British wanted to occupy New York, a more strategically located city. By the end of August the "redcoats," as the British soldiers were known, had easily captured New York's Manhattan Island and Long Island.

Philadelphians celebrating the Declaration of Independence

The British commander, Sir William Howe, offered the rebels a royal pardon that would save them from hanging if they would lay down their weapons. When Congress refused the pardon, Howe sent his soldiers marching toward Philadelphia. The congressional delegates quickly fled one 100 miles (160 km) south to Baltimore, Maryland.

Meanwhile, Jones received new orders from the Naval Committee. The orders instructed him to "protect, aid & assist all vessels & property belonging to these states or the subjects thereof. It is equally your duty to seize, take, sink, burn or destroy that of our enemies." These broad instructions gave Jones leeway to do whatever he thought best.

Despite his earlier apprehensions, Jones found that he liked the sloop. The *Providence* was just 70 feet (21 km) long and carried a crew of 73 men and boys. It was not heavily armed, with only 12 four-pound cannons. But the sloop was fast and nimble, as Jones soon learned.

On September 4, while sailing near British North America, the *Providence* met the Royal Navy's *Solebay*. Captain Jones knew that he was no match for the 26-gun frigate, so he decided to

flee. As the *Solebay* pulled alongside the
Americans, Jones could see the British tars
preparing to fire a broadside. He ordered his
helmsman to abruptly steer the sloop in front of
the *Solebay*'s bow, or front, and outrun the larger
ship. Before the *Solebay* could turn about, the
Providence had a long lead. The British chased the
Americans for ten hours before giving up. "Our
hairbreadth escape & the saucy manner of making
it," Jones later said, "must have mortified" the
British captain.

During the 49-day voyage, Captain Jones captured 16 British vessels. Captured ships were
called *prizes* because they were sold to govern-
ments or to wealthy merchants. The money paid
was shared by the officers and sailors who captured the prize. This was a popular practice in
America, Britain, France, and other countries.

Most nations allowed their captains and crews
to keep the entire prize money, but the Continental
Congress, always desperate for money, kept two-
thirds of it. Jones, who was constantly giving
advice on how to improve the Navy whether it was
asked for or not, urged more generous terms. "If
our enemies, with the best established and most

formidable navy in the universe," he reasoned in one letter, "have found it expedient to assign all prizes to the captors–how much more is such policy essential to our infant fleet." Congress later modified its policy, only keeping half of the prize money.

Jones made one more voyage that fall, as captain of the *Alfred*, to attack colliers, or coal ships, supplying fuel to General Howe's army in New York. Near Louisbourg, Nova Scotia, Captain Jones captured three colliers. Earlier on the same voyage, amid a winter gale, Jones also captured the *Mellish* and its cargo of 10,000 winter uniforms intended for British general John Burgoyne. Burgoyne's troops were marching from Canada to meet General Howe on the Hudson River and divide New York and New England from the eight colonies west of the river. Jones sent the warm uniforms to General Washington's army camped at Valley Forge, Pennsylvania.

Despite Jones's successful missions, Commodore Hopkins gave the *Alfred* to another captain who had more seniority. Hopkins did not assign the Scotsman a new ship because none were available. The British had quickly destroyed or captured many of the new frigates ordered by Congress the previous year.

Jones, eager for a ship, sought the patronage of Robert Morris, a wealthy Philadelphia merchant and one of Pennsylvania's nine congressional delegates. The captain, generous with his flattery, wrote that "accepting my correspondence is the greatest favor I could have aspired to."

Nor was the sea captain shy about criticizing men above him on the seniority list. "That such despicable characters should have obtained commissions as commanders in a navy is truly astonishing," he wrote to Joseph Hewes.

Jones's constant criticism and boasting created many enemies. "I have had so many complaints against Capt. Jones that I should be glad of your direction whether it will be best to call a court martial upon him or not," Commodore Hopkins wrote to John Hancock, president of the Continental Congress. Benjamin Franklin offered Jones advice on getting along with others. "Criticizing and censuring almost every one you have to do with, will diminish friends, increase enemies, and thereby hurt your affairs."

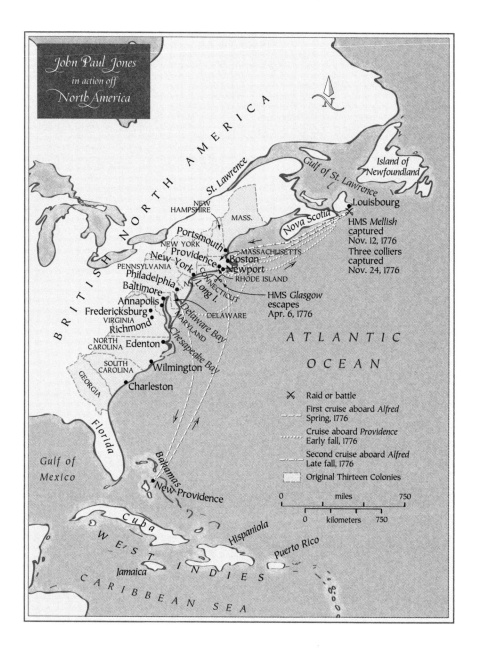

John Paul Jones
in action off
North America

St. Lawrence

Gulf of St. Lawrence

Island of
Newfoundland

B R I T I S H   N O R T H   A M E R I C A

NEW
HAMPSHIRE

MASS.

Nova Scotia

Louisbourg

HMS *Mellish*
captured
Nov. 12, 1776

Three colliers
captured
Nov. 24, 1776

Portsmouth

NEW YORK

Providence

New York

MASSACHUSETTS

Boston

Newport

RHODE ISLAND

CONNECTICUT

PENNSYLVANIA

Philadelphia

N.J.

Long I.

Baltimore

DELAWARE

Delaware Bay

HMS *Glasgow*
escapes
Apr. 6, 1776

Annapolis

Fredericksburg

VIRGINIA

Richmond

MARYLAND

Chesapeake Bay

NORTH
CAROLINA

Edenton

SOUTH
CAROLINA

Wilmington

A T L A N T I C

O C E A N

GEORGIA

Charleston

✕   Raid or battle

- - - -   First cruise aboard *Alfred*
Spring, 1776

········   Cruise aboard *Providence*
Early fall, 1776

— - —   Second cruise aboard *Alfred*
Late fall, 1776

Original Thirteen Colonies

Florida

Gulf of
Mexico

Bahamas

New Providence

0   miles   750

0   kilometers   750

Cuba

W E S T   I N D I E S

Hispaniola

Puerto Rico

Jamaica

C A R I B B E A N   S E A

While Jones had numerous critics, he also had powerful friends such as Franklin and Morris. "He is a fine fellow and should be constantly kept employed," Morris wrote to Hancock. Jones's supporters saw that Jones, unlike other American captains, was willing to take risks and engage the enemy rather than remain safely in port.

In the spring of 1777, Congress ordered Captain Jones to sail to France and take command of a man-of-war. A man-of-war was the largest fighting ship on the ocean. The Naval Committee also assigned Jones the *Ranger*, a 20-gun frigate under construction in New Hampshire. The *Journals of Congress* recorded the assignment on June 14, 1777. That day the *Journals* also recorded another memorable event:

"Resolved: That the flag of the thirteen United States be thirteen stripes, alternate red and white; that the union be thirteen stars, white in a blue field, representing a new constellation." Captain Jones would be flying the new American flag as he embarked on his most important assignment of the war. 🚢

Problems in Portsmouth

ONES TRAVELED TO PORTSMOUTH, New Hampshire, in July to pick up the *Ranger*. He hoped to cross the Atlantic Ocean and be in France by the end of summer. But problems with the ship's builder delayed his departure.

Portsmouth, a port on the Atlantic coast at the mouth of the Piscataqua River, was an old shipbuilding town. The first ship built in North America had been made there in 1690. Nearby forests supplied abundant oak trees for strong hulls and tall white pines for straight masts. Thirty carpenters could

A drawing of Portsmouth, New Hampshire, at about the time Jones lived there

build a frigate like the *Ranger* in a year. John Langdon, a local merchant and a former congressman and member of the Naval Committee, was overseeing the *Ranger's* construction on nearby Rising Castle Island, in the Piscataqua River.

Langdon, like Jones, had become a sea captain as a young man, at age 22. But the two men were very different in other ways. Langdon, six years older than Jones, was a fourth-generation American who had been born and raised on a New Hampshire farm. After being elected to the Second Continental Congress in 1775, Langdon used his office to secure contracts to build three frigates—the *Raleigh*, the *Ranger*, and the *America*—in his hometown.

In early 1776, the shipbuilder resigned his seat in Congress to buy and outfit seven privateers. These ships were making Langdon a wealthy man. Privateers, as the name suggests, were privately owned ships. They captured merchant ships belonging to other countries.

Privateers were both good and bad for America. They were good because the privateers hurt the British and helped the Americans by capturing

A portrait of John Langdon, who left Congress to make his fortune as a privateer.

ammunition and other precious supplies.
They were bad because the prize-seeking vessels
competed with the Continental Navy for men.

Sailors preferred going to sea on the prize-
seeking ships because they were less dangerous
and more profitable. Privateers never willingly
fought British men-of-war; they attacked only
poorly armed merchant ships. The privateers sold
their prizes–the captured ships and cargo–to the
government or to merchants. The captains and
owners of the privateers kept the biggest share of
the prize money, but each crewman received a
share, too. An estimated 20,000 men served on
approximately 2,000 American privateers during
the Revolution, while fewer than 5,000 men
served in the Continental Navy.

When Jones arrived in Portsmouth, he immediately went to inspect the *Ranger*. He did not
like what he saw. The ship's three masts were too
tall. They had been made for a bigger ship.
Oversize masts made a ship *crank*, or top-heavy,
and more likely to roll over in rough seas. Also,
the sails were made of hemp and jute, the material
used to make gunnysacks, rather than canvas,
which was stronger.

Langdon was in charge of buying stores for the voyage. The crew of 150 men would be at sea for a month or more. When Captain Jones learned that Langdon planned to supply the ship with only 30 gallons of rum, he complained, "This alone was enough to cause a mutiny." Sailing ships offered few comforts. Food and drink, Jones knew, were important to maintaining a crew's morale. When he last sailed the *Providence*, Jones stocked 600 gallons (2,300 l) of rum for a crew of 73 sailors. Drinking was a regular part of life on sailing ships. Each day, every man and boy on board a vessel received a ration of alcohol.

The captain was also unhappy with the officers who would be under his command. Langdon, with the help of another New Hampshire politician, William Whipple, picked the officers. The pair, indulging in what one historian called "localities," chose relatives and local men who would, in turn, support Langdon and Whipple in their political careers. They appointed Thomas Simpson, Langdon's brother-in-law, first lieutenant, the ship's second in command. They gave Lt. Samuel Wallingford, a Portsmouth man, command of the marines. Langdon and Whipple selected a total of ten local men to be officers on the *Ranger*. Their selections left Jones as the outsider and made his command more difficult.

To make matters worse, Langdon told the new officers that the *Ranger* would spend as much time pursuing prizes as fighting the enemy. This was not Captain Jones's plan, and his officers' eagerness for prizes would cause him trouble for months to come. If Jones had been a man who was solely bent on making money, as Langdon and others appeared to be, he could easily have made his fortune as a privateer. But he dismissed privateers as "licensed pirates."

Jones sent the Naval Committee numerous letters complaining about Langdon. It was an agent's job to supply a ship according to its captain's wishes, Jones wrote in one sarcastic letter, but "he thinks himself my master, and he, who was breed in a shop and hath been but a voyage or two at sea under a nurse, had once the assurance to tell me that he knew as well as myself how to fit out, govern and fight a ship of war!" And in another letter, he wrote, "The outfit of this small ship hath given me more anxiety and uneasiness than all the other duty which I have performed in the service."

Jones and Langdon became so angry with each
other that they scarcely talked.

Despite his anger with Langdon, Jones
enjoyed his months in Portsmouth. He lived in a
large white clapboard house owned by Sarah
Purcell, the widow of a ship's captain. This com-
fortable house made him dream of owning his
own home. Jones sent a letter to his friend Robert
Morris, asking him to use the captain's prize
money to purchase a "small landed estate" in
Virginia. He also designed a coat of arms for
himself with the slogan *Pro Republica*, a Latin
term that means "for the republic." It was a
public declaration of Jones's dedication to
American liberty.

The naval captain met several of the
town's single women. After leaving
Portsmouth, he wrote to John Wendell
and sent his compliments to "fair Miss
Wendell," the man's daughter, and to "the
other agreeable ladies of my acquaintance in
Portsmouth."

Jones also visited Boston, some 100 miles
(160 km) down the coast, where he became friends
with Phillis Wheatley. She was a former slave

*An 18th-century
engraving of the
Boston poet Phillis
Wheatley*

who had been freed by her master in 1773. Wheatley was a poet and a celebrity in Boston society. Jones had begun writing poetry of his own, and he wrote a poem for Wheatley, describing her as full of "beauty, harmony, and grace."

But Jones had little time to write poetry and socialize. Most of his energy was spent arguing with Langdon and searching the New England coast for crewmen. The captain gave an extra month's pay to sailors who signed up to serve on his ship. Some scoundrels signed on, collected their advances, and then shipped out on privateers. By fall, Jones had recruited 140 men. The sailors, like most ships' crews in that era, represented a variety of nationalities. There were Irishmen, French Canadians, Swedes, and two former slaves.

Early on the morning of November 1, the *Ranger* rode out of Portsmouth Harbor on the outgoing tide, which is called an ebb tide. The handsome frigate was painted black with a broad yellow stripe along its topside. It was 110 feet (33 m) from stern to bow, or back to front, slightly longer than a basketball court. It had three square-rigged masts and 18 nine-pound guns.

John Paul Jones raising the Stars and Stripes on the Ranger

A ship launching was cause for celebration. On the main deck, a drum and fife played while sailors climbed aloft, onto the spars, which were the ship's masts and yards, to adjust ropes and sails. Captain Jones stood on the poop deck, the small raised deck in the rear of the ship, dressed in his best navy, or dark blue, jacket, white knee breeches, and black tricornered hat. Hundreds of people gathered on shore to watch the new vessel ride the ebb tide out to sea.

New developments in the war made Jones especially eager to set sail. The captain wanted to reach France quickly so he would be the first to deliver important news that might persuade Louis XVI, the 23-year-old French king, to openly support the Americans. Two weeks earlier, on October 17, the Continental Army had defeated Gen. John Burgoyne at Saratoga, New York. The British general and all 5,000 of his soldiers had surrendered. It was one of the patriots' most important victories of the war. The news would be welcomed by the American commissioners– Franklin, Silas Deane, and Arthur Lee–who were in France's capital, Paris, seeking military support from that nation.

Crossing the Atlantic Ocean on a sailing vessel was difficult anytime, but more so in winter. "Hard gaile and dirty weather from the SE, blowing very hard and a large sea a-going. Ship abundance of water," Jones described the stormy weather and rough seas in the ship's log. The *Ranger* had no heat other than a small charcoal stove for cooking oatmeal, stew, and other simple meals.

The cold weather, one sailor explained, made the crew's work extra hard. "The running ropes freeze in the blocks; the sails are stiff like sheets of tin; and the men cannot expose their hands long enough to the cold, to do their duty aloft, so that topsails are not easily handled."

In a "large sea," no one stayed dry. As the ship tossed and turned, waves of salty seawater washed over the deck, streamed through cracks in the main deck, and soaked the sailors sleeping in their hammocks on the deck below. Despite the bad weather, *Ranger* made good time, arriving in France after 32 days, on December 2.

CHAPTER FIVE

Captain Jones Attacks Britain

WHEN CAPTAIN JONES WENT ASHORE at Brest, a seaport on France's northern coast, he was immediately disappointed, twice.

First, another American ship had arrived a day earlier with the news about the battle at Saratoga. That patriot victory would bring France into the war. French spies had learned that the British planned to offer the colonies a peace plan. Afraid the offer would ruin its opportunity to weaken its age-old rival Great Britain, France recognized the United States as a sovereign nation and

British troops surrendering after their defeat at Saratoga, New York

offered to supply money, arms, ships and soldiers.

Second, Jones learned that the French Navy had bought the ship he had expected to captain, the 44-gun man-of-war named *L'Indien*. He called it "one of the finest frigates that ever was built."

At Christmas, Jones visited Arthur Lee and Benjamin Franklin, two of the American commissioners in Paris. The commissioners told him to "proceed in the manner you judge best for distressing the enemy."

The *Ranger* sailed April 10 across the English Channel to Great Britain. Jones planned to capture British sailors to trade for American prisoners. He said he also wanted to "put an end to burnings in America by making one good fire in England of shipping."

Robert Morris and Jones had exchanged letters discussing naval strategy. "Our infant fleet cannot protect our own coasts," Morris wrote. "The only effectual relief it can afford us is to attack the enemies' defenseless places and thereby oblige them to station more of their ships in their own countries." Jones agreed with Morris. The captain would attack merchantmen and undefended ports to make

British people suffer the same hardships
Americans were suffering and, he hoped, pressure
their government to end the war.

Jones sailed to Whitehaven, the port in north-
west England where he had begun his career as a
sailor 17 years earlier. The captain did not feel any
malice toward the city. Rather, he decided to
attack this port simply because he knew it so well.

When the *Ranger*'s lookout saw the white
sandstone cliffs of St. Bees Head, a prominent
landmark south of Whitehaven, Captain Jones
told his crew of his plan to burn ships in the
harbor. Several officers argued for taking the best
vessels as prizes. Jones insisted the crew follow
his plan, but they had other ideas.

That evening a Swedish sailor, Edward Meyer,
Jones later reported to the Naval Committee, told
the captain of a plot to hijack the ship. This was
mutiny! Captain Jones hid two loaded pistols
under his jacket. Just after midnight, the raiding
party climbed into the cutters, which were small
boats with single sails. Jones grabbed one of the
mutiny's leaders and pointed a pistol at the
sailor's head. Mutineers come to an unhappy end,
he warned–ending this mutiny.

Jones and his men rowing ashore to burn the ships at Whitehaven, England

Captain Jones, along with Lieutenant Wallingford and 40 marines and sailors, reached Whitehaven harbor at daybreak. Jones estimated that 250 ships were anchored there. The captain led half the men quietly to the harbor's south end, while Wallingford took the other half to the north end.

"We took the fort by storm," Jones reported. "Lacking ladders, we had to climb it by mounting upon the shoulders of our largest and strongest men, and enter it in this manner through the embrasures. {Embrasures are openings in a wall.} I commanded this operation, and I was also the first who entered the fort. The morning was cold and the sentinels had retired to the guard-room; they were not expecting such a hostile visit. No blood at all was shed in securing their post; we spiked ⟨jammed the cannon barrels⟩ thirty-six cannon of the fort and battery. I advanced at length to the southern part of the harbor to burn all the ships there."

Jones thought the raid was working well until, "To my great astonishment, I saw that the boat sent to the northern part had returned without having accomplished anything. Those who had gone in it pretended to have been frightened by certain noises which they had heard, but I told them that these noises existed only in their imagination." It turned out that Lieutenant Wallingford's men had broken into a pub, or bar, and "made very free with the liquor."

Then, the captain heard shouting from town. A crewman, an Irishman named David Freeman, had deserted. He ran from house to house, banging on doors and yelling that pirates were burning the ships. Townspeople were swarming toward the harbor. Jones tossed a torch of brimstone-coated canvas onto a large merchantman.

Flames engulfed the wooden ship as the raiders rowed back to the *Ranger*.

"What was done," Jones explained, "is sufficient to show that not all their boasted navy can protect their own coasts and that the scenes of distress which they have occasioned in America may be soon brought home to their own doors." He was referring to the burning by redcoats of Norwalk, Connecticut, and of other New England towns.

Jones next sailed across Solway Firth, a broad inlet of the Irish Sea, to St. Mary's Isle. The captain planned to raid the estate of the Earl of Selkirk, a Scottish peer or nobleman, take the Earl hostage, and exchange him for American prisoners of war.

The *Ranger* dropped anchor near St. Mary's Isle late on the morning of April 18. Jones, Lieutenant Wallingford, Master's Mate David Cullam, and 12 marines rowed ashore. Walking up the path to the Earl's mansion, the raiders met a gardener who told them the nobleman was away in London.

Disappointed, Jones turned back toward the ship, but Cullam and Wallingford wanted to loot the mansion. After all, the pair argued, they had taken few prizes and it would boost morale. The captain reluctantly agreed, but he told them not to harm anyone, to take only household silver, and to show "the utmost respect."

Lady Selkirk later described that morning's events in a letter. The family was finishing breakfast when she saw "horrid looking wretches," outside the house. "Upon the whole, they behaved civilly. The men were each armed with a musket and bayonet, two large pistols and a hanger. {A hanger is a short sword.} The doors were open. None of them offered to come in, nor asked for anything."

After introducing themselves, Cullam and Wallingford explained they wanted the family's silver. "Wallingford seemed by nature very disagreeable," Lady Selkirk observed. He "had a vile blackguard look, but still kept civil as well as he might, but I suspect might have been rough enough had he met with provocation." She described Cullam as "a civil young man in a green uniform" who "seemed naturally well bred and not to like his employment."

Lady Selkirk told her butler to put the family's silver platters, pitchers, and other valuables in sacks. Meanwhile, she gave Wallingford and Cullam each a glass of wine and asked them to write a receipt for the silver. The officers complied, thanked Lady Selkirk for her hospitality, and left.

"At going off, they said that they belonged to the Ranger frigate, Captain John Paul Jones, Esq., commander," Lady Selkirk noted. "It was immediately known that this Paul Jones is one John Paul, born at Arbigland . . . a great villain as ever was born, guilty of many crimes and several murders by ill usage, was tried and condemned for one, escaped and followed a piratical life till he engaged with the Americans. He seems to delight in that still, as robbing a house is below the dignity of the States of America."

Cullam and Wallingford told the captain of Lady Selkirk's politeness. Her behavior impressed Jones. The captain wrote her a letter promising to return the silver. Jones also asked her "to use your soft persuasive arts with your husband to endeavor to stop this cruel and destructive war, in which Britain can never succeed." He sent the

The British called Jones a pirate. This caricature of him dates from the late 1770s.

silver back several years later, in 1784, and Lord
Selkirk gave accounts of Jones's chivalrous action
to the newspapers.

Although Jones knew warships were searching
for him, he did not rush back to the safety of
France. He sailed slowly along the Irish coast. On
April 24, the *Ranger*'s lookout spotted the Royal
Navy's *Drake* sitting in a bay called Belfast Lough.

The captain had passed the *Drake* while sailing
to Whitehaven. Then, a gale had prevented him
from attacking. Now, Jones had the enemy in his
sights once again.

The *Drake*'s captain, a man who history
knows only by his last name of Burden, saw the
Ranger, but he did recognize it as an American
ship. With its cannons hidden behind the closed
gun ports, the *Ranger* looked like a merchant ship.
Burden sent a lieutenant in a skiff to investigate.
Jones told his crew to hide quietly below deck.
Huddled in the *Ranger*'s hold, the men ques-
tioned the plan to attack the British ship.
Meanwhile, Captain Jones politely invited the
English lieutenant aboard, introduced himself,
and informed the visitor he was a prisoner. This
bold act amused Jones's crew. Suddenly, they

liked the idea of attacking the British warship.

When the lieutenant did not return, Burden suspected he had been taken prisoner and prepared to attack. The *Drake* took nearly an hour to sail out against the incoming tide. When the two vessels were within cannon shot, the *Drake*'s crew raised the red ensign of the Royal Navy and the *Ranger*'s crew raised the Stars and Stripes. The Ranger cannon fired a broadside of grapeshot. Jones did not want to sink the *Drake*, so he told his gunners to aim at the masts and sails.

"The battle was warm, close and obstinate," Captain Jones wrote. "It lasted an hour and four minutes when the enemy called for quarters; her fore and main-topsail yards being both cut away. The loss of the enemy was in killed and wounded forty-two men. The captain and lieutenant were among the wounded; the former, having received a musket ball in the head the minute before they called quarters." Blood and rum made the *Drake*'s deck slippery. A cannonball had smashed a keg of rum, which the English crew had opened expecting to celebrate a victory. Captain Burden and a first lieutenant named Dobbs had been killed. They "were buried with the honor due their rank," Jones

John Paul Jones
and the
Ranger

✕   Raid or battle

- - -   Route of the
Ranger

0   miles   150

0   km   150

ATLANTIC OCEAN

SCOTLAND

N

Apr. 26, 1778

GREAT

BRITAIN

Belfast Lough

Kirkcudbright

Solway Firth

N O R T H

Belfast

Estate raid

HMS *Drake*
defeated
Apr. 24, 1778

Whitehaven

S E A

*Isle of
Man*

Port raid
April 18, 1778

IRISH SEA

Dublin

Apr. 17, 1778

B R I T I S H   I S L E S

IRELAND

ENGLAND

Cork

St. George's Channel

WALES

London

April 14, 1778

Thames

NETHERLANDS

CELTIC SEA

Plymouth

E n g l i s h   C h a n n e l

May 5, 1778

Seine

Paris

Brest
Departure:
April 10, 1778
Return:
May 8, 1778

F R A N C E

noted, "and with the respect due their memory."

This battle was the most spectacular engage-
ment between the two navies to date. And it was a
rare victory of a Continental Navy vessel over a
Royal Navy ship of war.

On May 8, 1778, the *Ranger* and the captured *Drake* entered the harbor at Brest. Jones's
first venture had been a success, but it was hardly
enough to satisfy the ambitious captain.

The Bonhomme Richard

WHILE CAPTAIN JONES ENJOYED THE fear that he had created in the British Isles, he wanted to accomplish a feat that would bring him honor and glory. But first he needed a better ship. In a letter to Jacques-Donatien Leray de Chaumont, a wealthy Frenchman, Jones said, "I wish to have no connection with any ship that does not sail fast, for I intend to go in harm's way."

The captain constantly wrote to his contacts, asking for their help in securing a good ship. Jones sent letters to

Serapis *and* Bonhomme Richard *battle off Flamborough Head.*

Benjamin Franklin, to John Adams, and even to France's King Louis XVI. He appealed to George Washington by sending the general a pair of gilt epaulets, which are shoulder ornaments worn on a uniform. After several months, Jones became so frustrated that he began to accuse people of plotting against him. He called Adams, "Mr. Round face . . . a conceited and wicked upstart." This was unfair criticism because Adams was a loyal supporter.

In November 1778, the French finally found the captain a vessel that he liked. It was *Le Duc de Dura*, an old merchant ship four stories tall and nearly the length of a football field. It had a luxurious cabin for the captain along with a drawing room, a dining room, and a balcony with a gold balustrade, or decorative railing.

Jones converted the ship to a man-of-war by outfitting it with six nine-pound cannon, 28 12-pound cannon, and six 18-pound cannon. Then he renamed it *Le Bonhomme Richard*. This was a French translation of Franklin's pen name, "Poor Richard," which Franklin used writing his famous almanacs. It was a good choice. The French loved Franklin. So the name *Bonhomme Richard* pleased

Benjamin Franklin is introduced to King Louis XVI at Versailles.

two of the captain's most important benefactors, France and Franklin.

Jones's hardest task was finding a good crew. The captain needed men with specific skills, such as pilots who were familiar with the waters along Scotland and England. Searching the French ports, Jones eventually recruited 380 men and boys. It was a diverse group of Frenchmen, Irishmen, Italians, Norwegians, Portuguese, Scots, Swedes, and Swiss. There were 79 Americans, former prisoners of war who had been exchanged for British captives. Jones even took several dozen Englishmen from French jails.

The motley crew soon proved troublesome. "Henry Phipps and Thomas Harris confined for fighting; Massie, a French soldier, confined for desertion," Jones's noted in the ship's log. "They were generally so mean," the captain wrote, "that the only expedient I could find that allowed me to command was to divide them into two parties and let one group of rogues guard the other."

Jones had to replace the English sailors when he discovered their plot to capture him and the *Richard*. Jones turned the ringleader over to the French. A court convicted the sailor of mutiny and ordered the man flogged with 250 lashes of a cat-o'-nine-tails and locked away in a prison. Jones replaced the Englishmen with Portuguese sailors.

French and Spanish admirals wanted Captain Jones to participate in an ambitious plan to invade England. They asked the American officer to again raid northern England. The raid, the admirals believed, would cause the Royal Navy to send its best ships in pursuit of Jones. Meanwhile, the French and Spanish navies would land an invading army near England's capital, London. The problems with his crew delayed Jones's departure, but the French and Spanish admirals sent 64 ships with 40,000 French soldiers across the English Channel. The French fleet sailed in June, but the Spanish fleet did not join them until August. By then, thousands of French sailors and soldiers were sick with smallpox, scurvy, and typhus. The admirals called the invasion off.

Captain Jones finally set sail August 14. Because he commanded a group of ships called a squadron, the French government recognized him as "the Honorable Captain John P. Jones, Commander in Chief of the American Squadron now in Europe." His squadron consisted of *Bonhomme Richard*, *Alliance*, *Pallas*, and *Vengeance*.

By the time the American squadron reached Ireland, Captain Jones was again having problems with his crew. Seven sailors deserted, rowing ashore in a cutter and giving the British a detailed account of Jones's ships and mission.

This model of the Bonhomme Richard *was photographed at the U.S. Naval Academy.*

Trouble also developed with Pierre Landis, a Frenchman who had joined the Continental Navy. Landis was captain of the *Alliance*. He refused to obey orders or even to respond to signals from the *Richard*. Jones sent four officers to talk with the Frenchman. They reported that Landis "spoke of the Captain in terms highly disrespectful and insolent . . .{and said} he would see him {Jones} on shore when they must kill one or t'other." Jones could do little about the insubordinate Frenchman until he returned to France.

The fleet sailed to Leith, the port of Scotland's capital Edinburgh. Captain Jones planned to capture Leith and demand a ransom to spare the city from being sacked and burned.

Because of the deserters, news quickly spread along the coast that the notorious "pirate" John Paul Jones was prowling about. The British called Jones a pirate rather the more respectful title of captain. "The appearance of Paul Jones off our town continued for some days," one Englishman told an interviewer years later, "keeping us all on the alert and in the alarm." But Jones had his sights only on Leith.

As they sailed into the Firth of Forth, the wide ocean inlet where Leith is located, Jones tried to disguise his ships as Royal Navy ships. He ordered his fleet to fly Union Jacks–British flags– and the marines to put on red coats so they would look like British soldiers. The ruse fooled at least one resident, who thought the *Bonhomme Richard* was the British gun ship HMS *Romney*. (HMS stands for His Majesty's Ship.)

Sir John Anstruther lived in a mansion overlooking the harbor. He had a brass cannon, but no gunpowder or cannonballs. Anstruther saw the ships flying Union Jacks sailing up the Firth. Thinking they were Royal Navy Ships, he sent two servants in a skiff to borrow powder and shot. On board the *Richard*, Jones gave the men a barrel of gunpowder, but he did not have the right size cannonball. The captain asked one of the men to stay on board to help pilot the fleet through the channel. This obliging Scotsman later reported this exchange to a local newspaper.

"What's the news?" Jones asked the man.

"Why, that rebel and pirate Paul Jones is off the coast, and he ought to be hanged."

"Do you know whom you are addressing?"

"Are you not Captain Johnston of HMS *Romney*?"

"No, I am Paul Jones."

The man dropped to his knees and begged for mercy.

"Get up," Jones laughed. "I won't hurt a hair on your head, but you are my prisoner."

With the man's help, Jones and his squadron sailed up the Firth. Lookouts atop the walls of Edinburgh Castle, nearly a mile from the harbor, spotted the fleet. Not fooled by the British flags, the lookouts sounded the alarm with rolling drums, blowing bugles, and shrill pipes. The men in the city armed themselves with muskets, pikes, and claymores, which are double-edged broadswords.

The American fleet dropped anchor and the marines prepared to row ashore. But a sudden gale came blowing up the Firth. The wind blew so hard it nearly snapped the *Richard*'s masts. The gale died down by evening, but Captain Jones knew he had lost the element of surprise and cancelled the plan. It would have been quite a feat to capture Scotland's capital. But fate had a different feat in store for him. 🚢

The Big Battle

CAPTAIN JONES AND HIS FLEET CRUISED
slowly along England's Yorkshire coast.
They captured several colliers along the busy waterway and locked
their crews, about 100 men, in the hold below the gun deck.

On September 23, 1779, as the squadron neared
Flamborough Head, a promontory of white cliffs south of Robin
Hood's Bay, the *Bonhomme Richard*'s lookout saw dozens of sails
on the horizon. It was a fleet of ships sailing in their direction.
Word of the sighting ran through the excited crew like a jolt of

This dramatic painting depicts Captain Jones during the battle against the Serapis.

electricity. Men strained to catch glimpses of the fleet, some six miles (10 km) to the north.

The ships belonged to a convoy of some 60 merchantmen carrying naval supplies from Christiansund, Denmark, to the British dockyards in southern England, three days away. Two Royal Navy men-of-war, the *Countess of Scarborough* and *Serapis*, escorted the convoy. The *Serapis*, the larger of the two vessels, was under the command of Capt. Richard Pearson.

Captain Pearson did not know that he had met the enemy. As usual, the *Richard* and the other American ships were flying Union Jacks. But the British captain suspected trouble. That morning, the convoy had passed Scarborough Castle, where a big red flag had been raised above the gray walls. Towns along the coast raised red flags when enemy ships or pirates were nearby. Like a mother hen protecting her chicks, Pearson ordered his men to prepare for battle as he maneuvered the *Serapis* between the convoy and the suspicious ships. He fired a signal gun, warning the merchants to turn back to the harbor by Scarborough Castle, where they would be protected by the castle's big cannons.

As soon as Captain Jones saw the convoy he

John Paul Jones
and the
Bonhomme Richard

Shetland
Islands

September 4, 1779

Aug. 31,
1779

Orkney
Islands

ATLANTIC

OCEAN

Outer Hebrides

Inner Hebrides

SCOTLAND

NORTH

Firth of Forth

Leith

SEA

Edinburgh

GREAT

BRITISH

BRITAIN

Flamborough Head

Scarborough

USS Bonhomme
Richard sinks
Sept. 25, 1779

ISLES

Aug. 26,
1779

IRELAND

IRISH

HMS Serapis
defeated
Sept. 23, 1779

SEA

To Texel,
Netherlands

WALES

ENGLAND

CELTIC

Thames

London

NETHERLANDS

SEA

English Channel

Channel Islands

Seine

Paris

Route of the
Bonhomme Richard

0   miles   150

0   km   150

Lorient
Departure:
August 14, 1779

Île de Groix

FRANCE

decided to attack. He gave orders to hoist the flag that signaled "general chase" to his ships. Only a light wind blew over the calm sea, so it took the Americans several hours to come within hailing distance of the *Serapis*. Captain Jones briefed his men on the battle plan. The *Richard's* large guns, the 18-pound cannons, would fire into the *Serapis's* hull to sink the ship, while the 12- and 9-pound cannons would fire into the rigging and sails to try to disable it.

From a distance, Captain Pearson believed the 40-gun *Richard* was a two-deck, 64-gun ship, accompanied by its three frigates. His 44-gun *Serapis* and 20-gun *Countess* would be a poor match against such a force. But it was the British captain's duty to protect the convoy. No matter how strong his opponent, he would fight to give the supply ships time to escape.

By late afternoon, *Richard* was less than a mile (1.6 km) from *Serapis*. Drummers marched up and down the deck sounding "beat to quarters." Forty marines armed with muskets, blunderbusses, and grenades climbed to the round platforms, called "tops," high up on each of the three masts. Sailors put grappling hooks, pikes, hatchets, and swords within easy reach. The powder monkeys stacked roundballs, grapeshot, and cartridges next to the cannons. William Bannatyne, the surgeon, set up his operating table and sharpened his saws and knives as his assistants placed buckets nearby for amputated limbs.

As the sun slid behind Flamborough Head, Jones ordered his men to run up three blue-and-yellow flags. This was the signal for his squad to "form line of battle." The other three ships– *Alliance, Pallas,* and *Vengeance*–hung back. It was never clear whether they did not understand the order or simply chose to ignore it. Jones suspected the worst, that they were willfully avoiding the battle. *Bonhomme Richard* faced *Serapis* alone. Captain Jones's report described the events of that evening.

Slowly, the two ships drew closer. Pearson hoisted a big red ensign and nailed the bottom of the flag to the staff. This was a signal to his crew that the *Serapis* would never surrender.

When the two ships were less than 300 feet (90 m) apart, Jones remembered Captain Pearson shouting across the calm sea, "This is His Majesty's ship *Serapis.* What ship is that?"

"The *Princess Royal*," Jones responded,

naming a British merchant ship of similar size
to *Richard*.

"Where from?" Pearson asked.

"I can't hear what you say," Jones said, stalling
for time so he could get as close as possible.

"Tell me instantly from whence you came and
who you be or I'll fire a broadside into you,"
Pearson demanded.

Like a bulldog baring its teeth, the *Serapis*
raised its gun port lids, revealing two decks of cannons, 20 18-pound guns, 22 nine-pounders, and
two six-pounders. Jones then gave the signal to
raise the red, white, and blue American flag. A
marine on *Richard*'s main top fired his musket, as
though signaling the battle to begin. Flames leaped
from the cannons, and clouds of smoke filled the
air with the smell of black powder as both vessels
fired full broadsides.

Half of *Serapis*'s guns had been double-shotted,
or loaded with two cannonballs. An 18-pound
roundball fired from a distance of 300 feet (90 m)
away could easily go through both sides of a ship's
thick oak hull. That first broadside sent some 30
iron balls smashing through *Richard*'s hull, leaving
jagged holes at the waterline. *Richard*'s cannons,

double-shotted as well, fired more than 20 roundballs into *Serapis*'s hull.

Each crew quickly ran in its cannons,
sponged, loaded, rammed, primed, and ran them
out to fire second broadsides. The well-trained
British gunners won the race, blasting more holes
in *Richard*'s hull.

When *Richard*'s crew fired its second broadside, a violent explosion shook the whole ship.
Two cannons on the gun deck, which is one level
below the main deck, had exploded, killing several
men and badly burning dozens more. The explosion destroyed an entire battery of cannon and
left a gaping hole in the main deck. This freak
accident left *Richard* with only a single battery of
12-pound guns on its upper deck.

"The battle being thus begun was continued
with unremitting fury," Jones wrote. The *Serapis*,
the faster of the two ships, crossed *Richard*'s stern
several times, raking the American vessel with
roundballs and grapeshot. Several 18-pound
cannonballs crashed through the transom, tore
through the entire length of the upper deck, and
exited through the bow, leaving *Richard*'s stern in
shambles. Some 60 men were dead or dying

The Serapis *and* Bonhomme Richard *firing broad-sides*

aboard Jones's ship. Another 70 were writhing and screaming in agony from their wounds. Of the 25 marines stationed on the poop deck, only three escaped death or injury. "She made a dreadful havoc among our crew," Jones reported. "Our men fell in all parts of the ship by scores."

Jones realized it would be suicidal to continue this cannon duel. He stood a better chance by grappling and boarding. The two ships were only a few yards apart as their crews worked frantically to adjust the sails and maneuver in the light breeze. *Richard*, its hold filling with water, moved slowly.

Pearson took advantage of a gust of wind to ram the bow of his ship into *Richard*'s stern. Jones grabbed a rope dangling from the *Serapis* and lashed it around his own mizzenmast, which is the rear mast. The two ships now were locked together, stern to bow, in the shape of a V. The vessels slowly drifted together, starboard by starboard, cannon muzzles nearly touching.

"Well done my brave lads," Jones shouted to his crew. "We have got her now. Throw on board her the grappling-irons and stand by for boarding."

Pearson wanted to shake this deadly embrace. He ordered his men to cut or cast off the grappling hooks. A fierce fight ensued as the British sailors tried to sever the hooks and the Americans tried to stop them. The sharpshooters in *Richard's* tops picked off every tar who got near the hooks. The noise of musket fire, grenade explosions, cannon blasts, crackling fires, and curses of anger and pain filled the air.

A full harvest moon rose over the calm ocean. Onshore, nearly two miles (about 3 km) away, hundreds of people from the villages of Flamborough, Filey, Sewerby, and Speeton gathered on the grassy cliff tops to watch the deadly dual. To the onlookers, both ships must have appeared doomed. Flames from the gunpowder flashes had spread up the rope rigging to the canvas sails.

"The fire was, at this time, nearly all over both ships and even as high as their tops," Jones wrote. More seriously, a fire blazed between *Richard's* decks, near the room where the gunpowder was stored. If the flames reached the powder, the ship would be blown to pieces.

On board the *Serapis*, "We were on fire not less than ten or twelve times in different parts," Pearson recalled in his account of the battle.

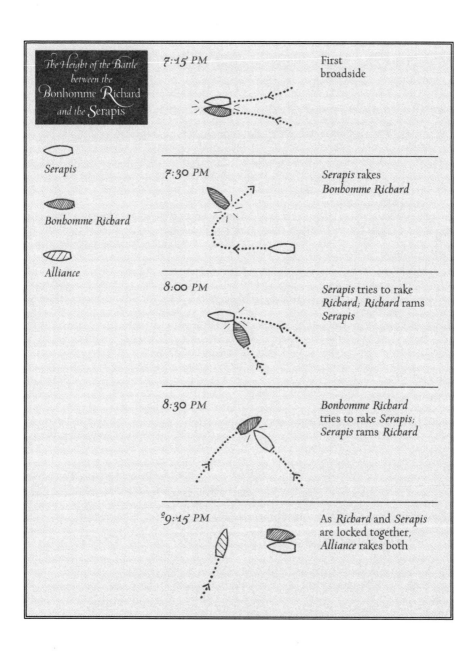

The Height of the Battle between the *Bonhomme Richard* and the Serapis

Serapis

Bonhomme Richard

Alliance

7:45 PM — First broadside

7:30 PM — *Serapis* rakes *Bonhomme Richard*

8:00 PM — *Serapis* tries to rake *Richard; Richard* rams *Serapis*

8:30 PM — *Bonhomme Richard* tries to rake *Serapis; Serapis* rams *Richard*

9:15 PM — As *Richard* and *Serapis* are locked together, *Alliance* rakes both

The fire on both ships became so bad that all
shooting stopped for a time so the crews could
put out the worst of the flames.

Several hundred yards (half a kilometer) away,
the *Pallas* engaged the *Countess of Scarborough*.
It was a short and uneven match. *Pallas* carried a
crew of 250 men and 26 eight-pound and six four-
pound cannons, whereas *Countess* had a crew of
420 men and 20 six-pounders. The two ships
fought for only one glass before *Pallas* completely
disabled *Countess*.

The 36-gun *Alliance* then finally joined the battle. Twice it sailed by *Serapis* and *Richard*, firing
broadsides of grapeshot and round shot into both
the British and the American ship. Before with-
drawing completely from the battle, *Alliance* made
a third pass, once again raking both vessels with
cannonfire. The broadsides killed and wounded
dozens of men on both sides. On *Richard*, one eye-
witness related, Midshipman Jonas Caswell
uttered, "*Alliance* has wounded me," and then died.

Richard's crew could fire only three of its 42-
pound guns, and they were aimed at the British
man-of-war's main deck. Captain Jones took
charge of these guns. He began firing one of them

repeatedly at the mainmast, hoping to topple it.

In *Richard's* hold the flooding became so severe that the master-at-arms released the terrified prisoners and ordered them to man the pumps. One prisoner climbed through a gun port and leaped over to the *Serapis*. He told Pearson to hold out a little longer because there was five feet (almost two meters) of water in the hold and *Richard* would surely sink soon.

The chief gunner, Henry Gardiner, and the chief carpenter, John Gunnisson, climbed up to the main deck to tell Captain Jones the ship was sinking. In the confusion and smoke, the two men could not find either Jones or the first lieutenant, Richard Dale. They assumed both men had been killed. If that was the case, Gardiner was the senior officer. Believing that the ship was going to sink, burn, or explode, he decided to surrender.

The two men ran to lower the ensign, crying "Quarters, quarters, our ship is sinking!" Jones, manning the cannon on the starboard side, heard their cry. He chased after the pair shouting, "Shoot them, kill them." The captain drew his pistol. It was empty. He flung the gun at Gardiner, hitting him in the head and knocking him unconscious.

Captain Pearson, just a few yards away on his own ship, heard the shouts and asked, "Have you struck? Do you call for quarters?"

This is where Jones supposedly replied, according to an early biography, "I have not yet begun to fight!" One sailor remembered him saying, "No, I'll sink, but I'll be damned if I strike!" In his report, Jones recalled only that he answered "in the most determined negative."

The fighting slowed as the crews listened to this exchange. When it became clear the Americans had not surrendered, the fighting resumed at a furious pace.

"Boarders away!" the British captain shouted as dozens of his men armed with cutlasses and pikes climbed over the bulwarks, or ship's sides. But, Pearson recounted, "They discovered a superior number lying under cover with pikes in their hands ready to receive them, on which our people retreated instantly into our own ship, and returned to their guns again."

The battle had been raging for nearly seven and a half glasses when one of *Richard's* crew, a Scot named William Hamilton, took several baseball-size grenades and climbed out on a yard that hung over the *Serapis*'s main deck. He dropped a grenade through an open hatch, down onto the gun deck, where six-pound cartridges of black powder were stacked. The exploding grenade ignited the powder and set off a chain of explosions the length of the gun deck. The covered deck was crowded with crewmen seeking safety from the sharpshooters in *Richard*'s tops. The blast killed at least 20 sailors instantly. Dozens of others, their clothing and hair in flames, jumped screaming through the gun ports into the sea.

The big blast barely fazed Captain Jones. He single-mindedly kept firing his cannon at the *Serapis*'s mainmast. Finally, a shot cracked the 150-foot (46 m) mainmast and caused it to lean to port, held up only by the web of rope rigging. Pearson then lost his nerve. He ran out onto the top deck and ripped down the ensign. He surrendered.

Lieutenant Dale led a boarding party onto the *Serapis* to take charge of the ship. When Captain Jones came aboard, Dale introduced him to Captain Pearson. The defeated Englishman handed the victorious American his sword. But Jones

returned it and invited the captain to his cabin
for a glass of wine.

The timbers on *Richard*'s lower deck, Jones
later wrote, "were mangled beyond my power of
description, and a person must have been an eye
witness to form a just idea of this tremendous
scene of carnage, wreck and ruin that every
where appeared. Humanity cannot but recoil
from the prospect of such finished horror. And
lament that war should be capable of producing
such fatal consequences."

There has never been an exact count of the
casualties, which were extraordinarily high for a
naval battle in that era. Estimates place the
number of dead and wounded at nearly 300 men,
roughly half of all of the crewmen on the two
ships. Nathaniel Fanning, a midshipman aboard
the *Bonhomme Richard*, later wrote of seeing "the
dead lying in heaps." He also described sailors
whose clothing, hair, and skin had been badly
burned. "The flesh of several of them dropped off
from their bones and they died in great pain."

CHAPTER EIGHT

After the Battle

OR A DAY AND A HALF, SOME 300 SAILORS from the American and British ships bailed seawater from the *Richard*'s hold as carpenters tried to plug the worst holes. But they could not save the ship. The crew carried the wounded men to the *Serapis*. From there, with "inexpressible grief," Captain Jones watched *Richard* disappear bow-first into the North Sea.

Pearson, although now a prisoner on his own ship, had done his job of protecting the valuable convoy. The ships were huddled safely in Scarborough's harbor. The owners of the merchantmen

An artist imagines flames consuming the Serapis *and* Richard.

later showed their gratitude when the British captain returned to England by awarding him a valuable silver vase. And King George III made him a knight, so he was forever after known as Sir Richard. Upon hearing that his former foe had been knighted, Captain Jones wrote to a friend, "Let me fight him again and I'll make him a lord." A lord, as a member of British nobility, is a higher rank.

Jones did not dwell long on his victory because he knew that the Royal Navy would be in hot pursuit of his squadron, so he sailed directly to the island of Texel, a neutral Dutch port. British warships followed and dropped anchor outside the port, expecting to capture the Americans when they eventually sailed to France or America.

French Navy officers took command of the *Serapis*, and Jones took over the *Alliance*. Benjamin Franklin had relieved Captain Landis of the *Alliance* because of his reckless behavior at Flamborough Head. The following year, the U.S. Navy would court-martial Landis and expel him from the service.

Jones remained in the Texel until December 1779. Then, during a gale, he slipped the *Alliance* past the waiting British ships and returned safely

to the French port of Lorient. Soon after dropping
anchor, Jones received orders from Franklin to
take urgently needed muskets, ammunition, and
uniforms to General Washington. But first,
before returning to America, the captain had to
appease his crew. The sailors had not been paid
for months, and they were angry. Jones traveled
to Paris to collect prize money that the government owed his men.

Parisians greeted the naval captain as a hero.
"Scarce anything was talked of at Paris and
Versailles," Franklin told him, "but your cool
conduct and persevering bravery during the terri-
ble conflict." The celebrated captain drank and
dined with dukes, counts, and barons. King Louis
XVI awarded him the Order of Military Merit,
one of France's highest honors. The king also
made Jones a *chevalier*, or French knight, and gave
him a sword with a beautiful gold hilt.

"The famous Paul Jones dines and sups here
often," wrote Caroline Edes, an Englishwoman
living in Paris. "He is a smart man of thirty-six,
speaks but little French, appears to be an extraor-
dinary genius, a poet as well as a hero. He is greatly
admired here, especially by the ladies, who are all

Jones's Order of
Military Merit, awarded
by the French king,
can be seen at the U.S.
Naval Academy
Museum.

wild for love of him, as he for them." Jones spent several happy months in Paris before he managed to collect a portion of his crew's prize money. A year after the victory at Flamborough Head, Jones at last set sail for America.

After a long, stormy voyage, the *Alliance* arrived in Philadelphia on February 18, 1784. British troops had withdrawn from the city several months earlier. In the three years that Jones had been away, the states had nearly finished ratifying the Articles of Confederation. The Articles established Congress as the new nation's central government.

Several congressmen, eager to honor the returning hero, wanted to promote the captain to rear admiral. He would have been the American Navy's first officer to hold that high rank, but other captains jealous of Jones's success blocked the promotion. The nation would not have its first rear admiral until David Farragut, the Union Navy's commander during the Civil War. Instead, Congress gave Jones command of a new frigate, *America*, a 74-gun battleship that was easily the finest, and virtually the only, vessel in the Continental Navy. The British had destroyed or captured all but two of the Navy's frigates. Jones planned to return to France in the man-of-war and lead an invasion of England.

But Congress soon disappointed Jones again. It abruptly gave *America* to the French to replace a man-of-war that had accidentally sunk in Boston Harbor. The ship proved to be a poor gift. *America* had been so badly constructed it had to be scrapped only four years later.

The year 1784 proved crucial in the war. British forces, under the command of Gen. Charles Cornwallis, had invaded the Southern colonies for the first time three years earlier. Cornwallis expected the South's many Tories to join his forces. Instead, he met stiff resistance.

Nathanael Greene, a former Quaker blacksmith from Rhode Island, led the American forces in the South. In January 1784, Greene dealt serious blows to the British in North Carolina, first at Cowpens and two months later at Guilford Courthouse. That summer, Cornwallis marched his troops north from Wilmington, North Carolina, to Yorktown, Virginia, on the lower Chesapeake Bay.

General Washington moved decisively. He coordinated strategy with his French allies, the

Cornwallis surrenders at Yorktown, Virginia, in 1781, ending the fighting in the American Revolution.

Comte (Count) de Rochambeau, who commanded the French land forces, and Adm. Comte de Grasse, commander of the French fleet. That fall, a combined army of French and American soldiers marched against Cornwallis's 7,000 redcoats camped in Yorktown, awaiting evacuation by the Royal Navy. French ships in the Chesapeake blocked the British rescue. Realizing that he was trapped, General Cornwallis surrendered on October 17, 1781. This effectively ended the war, although the formal treaty, the Treaty of Paris, would not be signed until September 3, 1783.

Jones returned to France in late 1783 as the American agent in charge of collecting unpaid prize money from the French government. But he longed for military action, and he traveled Europe looking for a navy to serve. The captain in 1788 accepted a commission as rear admiral in Russia's navy after that nation went to war with Turkey. It was not unusual for professional military men to serve in foreign armies or navies when their own nations were at peace. But Jones soon argued with the Russian military advisers, gave up his commission, and returned to Paris in May 1790.

For the next two years, the Revolutionary War hero lived in an apartment on rue de Tournon and did little other than see old friends and attend dinner parties. One evening, Jones met Lord Daer, the son of the Earl of Selkirk, at a dinner where the two men reminisced warmly about the raid on St. Mary's Isle years earlier.

France had changed a great deal after the French Revolution of 1789. The privileged Old Regime, as the king and the aristocracy were called, had lost its power. Jones, the *chevalier*,

The Order of St. Anne is housed at the U.S. Naval Academy. It's the gold metal Catherine the Great awarded John Paul Jones for his service in the Russian Army.

had been popular with the Old Regime but not with the new. Thomas Carlyle, an English writer and historian, met the American in Paris and described him in an essay. "In faded naval uniform, Paul Jones lingers visible here; like a wine skin from which the wine is drawn. Like the ghost of himself!"

In the summer of 1792, Jones became ill. His legs and stomach swelled up like balloons. He skin turned yellow with jaundice. Doctors could not identify or cure the illness. On July 18, 12 days after his 45th birthday, Jones died in his apartment on the rue de Tournon.

The responsibility for funeral arrangements fell to American officials. Gouverneur Morris, the American minister to France, ordered him buried in a pauper's grave. But the French government stepped in to save Jones from a poor man's burial by paying for the funeral. The government even paid extra to preserve the body by sealing it in a lead coffin filled with alcohol.

Dozens of French dignitaries attended the funeral, along with a detachment of Parisian policemen, old sailors, neighborhood shopkeepers, and residents. The dignitaries rode in carriages

behind the horse-drawn hearse, while the other people in the funeral procession walked the four miles (6.5 km) through the streets of Paris and into the nearby countryside to the Protestant cemetery. They arrived at dusk. As workers lowered the heavy lead coffin into the grave, the grenadiers, or honor guards, raised their rifles and fired a single volley into the air. The mourners then returned to the city in the last light of day. 🚢

John Paul Jones lived his last years in the Paris apartment building on the left.

CHAPTER NINE

Return to America

*I*NTELLECTUALS SUCH AS JAMES FENIMORE Cooper and Herman Melville kept the memory of John Paul Jones alive in novels, poems, and plays. And another intellectual, Theodore Roosevelt, America's 20th president, brought Captain Jones back to America.

In 1901, after the assassination of President William McKinley, Vice President Roosevelt became president of the United States. He was eager to impress the world with America's growing power. The new president, an avid naval historian, knew

President Theodore Roosevelt spoke at the ceremony for John Paul Jones in 1906.

all about John Paul Jones. He encouraged Gen. Horace Porter, the American ambassador to France, to find Jones's body, buried more than 100 years earlier.

This life-size bust of John Paul Jones at the U.S. Naval Academy is by Jean-Antoine Houdon.

A team of researchers studied old maps and documents to locate Jones's grave. The Protestant cemetery no longer existed. The growing city of Paris now sprawled over the old cemetery, and apartment houses, a laundry, and other buildings stood on top of the graves.

In 1905, workmen wielding picks and shovels descended into the basement of a laundry and began digging. They first dug up a stack of skeletons believed to be those of Swiss guards killed in August 1792, while trying to protect the King during the bloody second French Revolution, a period of violence when Louis XVI was beheaded and some 40,000 other French people were killed. The bodies of the Swiss guards had been unceremoniously tossed into a mass grave. Next, they found three lead coffins. Two contained the remains of civilians. But the third held Jones's body, remarkably well preserved, right down to his oddly shaped earlobe.

Roosevelt ordered the hero's body brought to America amid a splendid display of military prowess. In Paris, an honor guard of 500 French soldiers and U.S. Navy men, chosen because they were all more than six feet (183 cm) tall, escorted the flag-draped coffin along the Champs Élysées. The procession stopped at Les Invalides, where France's last emperor, Napoléon Bonaparte, was entombed. Diplomats and statesmen made speeches in honor of Jones. Afterward, a special train took the casket to the port town of Cherbourg.

The sailors solemnly carried the casket onto the American cruiser *Brooklyn*. It steamed across the Atlantic Ocean, escorted by three other cruisers, *Tacoma*, *Chattanooga*, and *Galveston*. In the previous 50 years, steamships had replaced sailing ships. The squadron crossed the Atlantic in 13 days, less than half of the time it had taken the old sailing ships. Seven steel-gray battleships joined the four cruisers for the final leg of the trip to the Chesapeake Bay and the U.S. Naval Academy at Annapolis, Maryland. Jones had arrived at his final resting place, where he would occupy a crypt in the new Naval Academy

John Paul Jones's crypt at the U.S. Naval Academy

Chapel, which was modeled after the grand cathedrals of Europe.

Today, Jones's accomplishments appear modest. But he deserves his place among America's Revolutionary War heroes. While other naval captains stayed safely in port to avoid danger or sought to get rich as privateers, Jones marshaled his scarce resources and sailed bravely into battle.

It was a matter of honor. Safety and personal fortune were less important to Jones than his duty of serving his adopted home.

On April 24, 1906, the anniversary of the *Drake*'s capture 128 years earlier, President Theodore Roosevelt spoke at the ceremony dedicating the naval hero's crypt. An American flag covered Jones's coffin. On top of the flag a wreath of laurel and a spray of palm lay beside the gold-hilted sword that King Louis XVI gave Jones when he made him a knight after capturing the *Serapis*.

John Paul Jones showed us, President Roosevelt said, that "he who would win glory and honor for the nation and for himself must not too closely count the odds."

The ceremonial sword given to Jones by the King of France is on display at the U. S. Naval Academy Museum.

Timeline

Entries in black are events in the life of John Paul Jones.
Entries in brown are key events in the American Revolution.

July 6, 1747	John Paul is born in Kirkcudbright, Scotland.
1761	John Paul at age 13 first visits Virginia.
1773	After killing a sailor during an argument aboard the *Betsy*, Captain John Paul assumes a new name and flees to North America.
December 16, 1773	Boston Tea Party.
Fall 1774	First Continental Congress calls for a boycott of trade with Great Britain.
December 1774	John Jones arrives in Virginia.
April 19, 1775	Battles of Lexington and Concord.
May 1775	Second Continental Congress meets in Philadelphia.
June 1775	The Second Continental Congress creates the Continental Army and appoints George Washington commander.
June 17, 1775	Battle of Bunker Hill, the first big battle of the American Revolution.
Summer 1775	General Washington arms eight New England fishing schooners. John Jones travels to Philadelphia and changes his name again.
October 30, 1775	The Continental Congress approves a resolution creating the Continental Navy.
November 10, 1775	The Continental Congress creates the Marines.
December 7, 1775	The Naval Committee enlists John Paul Jones, gives him the rank of lieutenant, and assigns him the task of outfitting the *Alfred*.
February 1776	The *Alfred* makes its maiden voyage as a warship.
March 1776	American ships raid New Providence, Bahamas.
April 1776	American ships engage the British warship *Glasgow*.
May 1776	John Paul Jones promoted to captain of the *Providence*.
July 1776	The colonies declare independence.
August 1776	The British capture New York. The *Providence* sails to the Caribbean, then to Canada.
September 4, 1776	The *Providence* escapes the Royal Navy's *Solebay*.
October 1776	The *Providence* returns to Narragansett Bay, having captured 16 British vessels.
November 1776	John Paul Jones, aboard the *Alfred*, captures three coal ships and the *Mellish*, a British ship carrying 10,000 winter uniforms.
Spring 1777	The Naval Committee assigns Jones the *Ranger* and orders him to France to take command of a newly built man-of-war.
June 14, 1777	The new flag of the United States is adopted.
October 17, 1777	The Continental Army defeats Gen. John Burgoyne at Saratoga, New York.
November 1, 1777	The *Ranger* leaves Portsmouth, New Hampshire, for France.
November 1777	The Continental Congress adopts the Articles of Confederation. The Articles go to the 13 states for ratification.
December 2, 1777	The *Ranger* arrives in France.

February 6, 1778	France formally recognizes the United States as a sovereign nation and greatly expands its assistance with the war.
April 10, 1778	Jones sails the *Ranger* to northern England.
April 18, 1778	Jones's attack on the port of Whitehaven is foiled by a deserter. He sails to St. Mary's Isle and loots the estate of the Earl of Selkirk, a Scottish peer.
April 24, 1778	The *Ranger* captures the British ship *Drake*.
May 8, 1778	Jones and the *Ranger* return to France.
November 1778	Jones outfits *Le Bonhomme Richard*.
December 1778	British general Charles Cornwallis invades the Southern colonies.
August 14, 1779	Jones, in *Richard*, sets out for Leith, the port city for the Scottish capital of Edinburgh.
September 23, 1779	*Richard* captures the Royal Navy man-of-war *Serapis* off Flamborough Head, England, and then sails to the Texel, a neutral Dutch port.
December 1779	Jones returns to France where he is made a chevalier, or French knight.
October 1780	Jones sets sail for America to deliver supplies to the Continental Army.
January 1781	Nathanael Greene and his American forces deal serious blows to the British in North Carolina, first at Cowpens and later at Guilford Courthouse.
February 18, 1781	After a long, stormy crossing, Jones arrives in Philadelphia.
March 1781	The Articles of Confederation go into effect after the last state, Maryland, ratifies them.
Summer 1781	Cornwallis marches his troops north from Wilmington, North Carolina, to Yorktown, Virginia.
October 17, 1781	Cornwallis surrenders, effectively ending the war.
September 3, 1783	The Treaty of Paris, the formal end to the war, is signed.
Late 1783	Jones returns to France as the American agent in charge of collecting unpaid prize money from the French government.
Spring 1788	Jones accepts a commission as rear admiral in Russia's navy during its war with Turkey.
May 1790	Jones returns to Paris.
July 18, 1792	Jones dies in his Paris apartment.
1901	Theodore Roosevelt becomes president of the United States and urges the American ambassador to France to find Jones's body.
April 1905	Jones's body, preserved in its lead casket, is found. The body is brought to America with great military pomp. Jones's final resting place is the U.S. Naval Academy at Annapolis, Maryland.
April 24, 1906	Theodore Roosevelt charges midshipmen at the U.S. Naval Academy with knowing the deeds of John Paul Jones.
Summer 2005	One hundred years after John Paul Jones's body arrived at Annapolis, his crypt is closed, refurbished, and reopened to the public with great ceremony.

Words & Expressions from the Days of Sailing Ships

Sailing ships were a major part of life in Great Britain, America, and other countries for several hundred years. It's not surprising that sailing terms have survived as common expressions. Here are a few examples.

Anchor	A ship's anchor is a heavy piece of iron that is lowered to the ocean floor to keep a boat or ship in place. Today, the word can also mean to simply keep in place or provide a sense of stability.
Ebb and flow	The phrase refers to the ocean tides coming in and going out, from high tide to low tide. But it's also an expression that refers, somewhat poetically, to anything that comes and goes, such as the ebb and flow of passion.
Hardtack	This was a hard, thin, unsalted bread or biscuit that was a staple on ships because it lasted for months. The phrase today can refer to any unappetizing or basic food.
Heavy or rough seas	This expression once literally referred to stormy seas, which made sailing difficult and dangerous. Today, it is also used to refer to any kind of difficult situation.
Keelhaul	Back in the days of sailing ships, this was just one more harsh punishment inflicted on sailors. A man was tied to a rope and dragged under water from one side of a boat's keel, or hull, to the other. Today it's a tongue-in-cheek expression for much less severe punishment.
Loose cannon	This phrase refers to an indiscreet or unpredictable person. In the days of sailing ships, iron cannons weighed hundreds of pounds. They were mounted on wheeled carriages and lashed in position. But if one got loose on the deck of a swaying vessel, it would roll back and forth, crashing into the wooden sides or into the wooden masts or flattening some hapless sailor. A loose cannon could be very destructive.
Lower the boom	Today, this expression refers to some unpleasant action. A boom is a heavy piece of wood that extends perpendicularly from the mast to hold the bottom part of a sail. The boom swings only a few feet above the deck, so sailors have to be prepared to dodge the boom when the position of the sail changes. Sailors who are not alert could be knocked unconscious or knocked into the water by the heavy boom.
Round robin	This phrase once referred to a type of petition in which sailors who were afraid of their captain expressed their grievances by signing their names, or making their marks, in a circle so that it was not obvious who signed first. Today, the expression is often used in sports in which every player or team plays against every other player or team.

Source Notes

Chapter One

Many of the details about John Paul Jones's early life are from Samuel Eliot Morison's *John Paul Jones: A Sailor's Biography* (New York: Little, Brown and Company, 1959). Morison brought two special talents to this long biography, his training as a naval officer and his training as a historian at Harvard University. The historian spent years researching Jones's life. Morison's descriptions of sailing and the sea were especially helpful to this landlubber author. Another helpful biography was Lincoln Lorenz's *John Paul Jones: Fighter for Freedom and Glory* (Annapolis, MD: Naval Institute Press, 1943). More recently, Evan Thomas published a readable biography, *John Paul Jones: Sailor, Hero, Father of the American Navy* (New York: Simon & Schuster, 2002).

Chapter Two

There is frustratingly little information on William Paul, John's brother, in Fredericksburg, Virginia, or on Jones's activities in that colony. But it was a big colony, full of Revolutionary War leaders, so there are many books about Virginia and its prominent citizens in the years leading up to the American Revolution. I dipped into Edward Countryman's *The American Revolution* (New York: Hill + Wang, 1985) as well as John E. Selby's *The Revolution in Virginia, 1775-1783* (Williamsburg, VA: Colonial Williamsburg Foundation, 1988). And Willard Sterne Randall's *George Washington* (New York:

Henry Holt, 1997) helped me understand the colony's class structure and revolutionary mood.

Chapter Three

There are plenty of books to read about the Declaration of Independence and the Second Continental Congress in Philadelphia. For a general overview of the time and place, I reread the relevant chapters in my favorite textbook, Alan Brinkley's *American History* (New York: McGraw-Hill, eighth edition, 1991). I found Russell Freedman's book for young readers *Give Me Liberty: The Story of the Declaration of Independence* (New York: Holiday House, 2000) valuable for its vivid detail. Several trips to Philadelphia also helped me understand the city and its history. My knowledge of the new Navy was aided by Gardner Weld Allen's *A Naval History of the American Revolution* (Williamstown, MA: Corner House Publishers, 1990). John Harland's *Seamanship in the Age of Sail* (Annapolis, MD: Naval Institute Press, 1984) supplemented Morison's descriptions to help me understand the many skills needed to sail a ship.

Chapters Four, Five, and Six

The information in the chapters about Jones at Portsmouth, his first months in Europe, and the *Bonhomme Richard* come from Lorenz, Morison, and Thomas biographies as well as from ship logs and Jones's letters and reports to the Naval Committee. *The Papers of John Paul Jones*, James C.

Bradford, editor (Alexandria, VA: Chadwyck-Healey, 1986) is on microfilm in the manuscript division of the Library of Congress. Some of Jones's letters are located in the manuscript collections of the men he corresponded with, such as Richard Dale and Benjamin Franklin.

Chapter Seven

Each of the biographies describes the battle off Flamborough Head in detail. I also consulted Jean Boudriot's *John Paul Jones and the Bonhomme Richard* (Annapolis, MD: Naval Institute Press, 1987). And I scanned the handy volume edited by John S. Barnes, *The Logs of the Serapis, Alliance, Arial under the Command of John Paul Jones, 1779-1780* (New Haven, CT: Naval History Society, 1961).

Chapters Eight and Nine

The final chapters of Jones's life are informed mainly by Morison's, Thomas's, and Lorenz's biographies. Another helpful source was *John Paul Jones last cruise and final resting place the United States Naval academy* {sic}, by H. (Henri) Marion (Washington, DC: G. E. Howard, 1906). This booklet describes the discovery and reburial of Jones's body. Marion's account includes lots of good detail about the ceremonies in Paris and in Annapolis. A visit to the Naval Academy is indispensable, as well as fun, to see artifacts from Jones's life and to see models of the Revolutionary-era ships.

Further Reading

Abigail Adams: Witness to a Revolution, Natalie S. Bober (New York: Atheneum, 1995).

The Amazing Life of Benjamin Franklin, James Cross Giblin (New York: Scholastic Press, 2000).

George versus George: The American Revolution as Seen by Both Sides, Rosalyn Schanzer (Washington, DC: National Geographic, 2004).

Give Me Liberty! The Story of the Declaration of Independence, Russell Freedman (New York: Holiday House, 2002).

A History of US: From Colonies to Country, Joy Hakim (New York: Oxford University Press, 1993).

If You Were There in 1776, Barbara Brenner (New York: Simon & Schuster, 1994).

Independence Now: The American Revolution, 1763-1783, Daniel Rosen (Washington, DC: National Geographic, 2004).

John Paul Jones: America's First Sea Warrior. Joseph F. Cullo (Annapolis, MD: Naval Institute Press, 2006).

John Paul Jones: Sailor, Hero, Father of the American Navy, Evan Thomas (New York: Simon & Schuster, 2002).

Thomas Jefferson: Architect of Democracy, John B. Severance (New York: Clarion Books, 1998).

Places to Visit in Person & by Internet

The U.S. Naval Academy in Annapolis, Maryland, hosts John Paul Jones Day the first or second Saturday of each July. The morning ceremony includes fife and drum performances, gun demonstrations, and period costumes.

The U.S. Naval Academy Museum has paintings, sculptures, and other exhibits pertaining to John Paul Jones and to the American Revolution.

The John Paul Jones Crypt in the U.S. Naval Academy Chapel underwent renovation in early 2005 and is once again open to visitors.

The Nimitz Library at the academy has a letter from George Washington to John Paul Jones and a letter from Jones to a newspaper editor. They can be read online at www.usna.edu/LibExhibits/JohnPaulJones/Jpj_main.html

John Paul Jones Cottage Museum, Dumfries, Scotland, the cottage where he was born, is now a museum open from April to September. www.jpj.demon.co.uk/visit.htm

The John Paul Jones House in Portsmouth, New Hampshire has an extensive collection of memorabilia and many links to related sites. http://seacoastnh.com/Maritime_History/John_Paul_Jones/John_Paul_Jones/

One of the world's largest nonprofit scientific and educational organizations, the National Geographic Society was founded in 1888 "for the increase and diffusion of geographic knowledge." Fulfilling this mission, the Society educates and inspires millions every day through its magazines, books, television programs, videos, maps and atlases, research grants, the National Geographic Bee, teacher workshops, and innovative classroom materials. The Society is supported through membership dues, charitable gifts, and income from the sale of its educational products. This support is vital to National Geographic's mission to increase global understanding and promote conservation of our planet through exploration, research, and education.

For more information, please call 1-800-NGS-LINE (647-5463)
or write to the following address:
National Geographic Society
1145 17th Street N.W.
Washington, D.C. 20036-4688
U.S.A.

Visit the Society's Web site: www.nationalgeographic.com